Thank You

CRAIG J. BOYKIN

MY LIFE, **YOUR** INSPIRATION

HOW TO TURN MINOR SETBACKS, INTO A MAJOR COMEBACK!

AN INSPIRATIONAL JOURNEY FROM GED TO PhD

My Life, Your Inspiration
How to Turn Minor Setbacks into a Major Comeback
An Inspirational Journey from GED to Ph.D.

www.mylifeyourinspiration.com

ISBN 978-0-615-86860-8

I want to hear from YOU!
I gladly welcome comments on how this book has helped you.
Please email me today at craigjboykin@gmail.com to leave
your feedback. Also comment on Facebook
at https://www.facebook.com/craig.boykin

Printed in the United States of America
Designed by: www.pencilworx.com

Disclaimer-
The purpose of this book is to inspire and motivate. The author and publisher shall have neither liability nor responsibility for anyone with respect to any loss or damage caused, directly or indirectly, by the information contained in this book.

Table of Contents

My Life, **FOREWORD**

By Dr. Lisa Cothran, Ph.D.

Professor of Psychology,
Alabama State University

"Don't you set down on the steps 'cause you finds it's kinder hard. Don't you fall now…" (Langston Hughes, 1902-1967)

As a social and personality psychologist who studies and conducts research on the psychology of Black Americans, I am well versed in the unique perceptions and realities of black adolescents and adults. So the first time I met Craig J. Boykin I thought to myself, "This guy's life story is impressive, he defies the stereotype of the young black American man." In Boykin's hard-hitting memoir, this son of an abused, drug-addicted mother and absent father presents an autobiographical example of faith and tenacity. He chronicles an accessible exposition of the common, precarious experiences of America's black boys and men.

Every unfortunate statistic that is more common to this group has been a pernicious part of Boykin's life: exposed to physical and verbal abuse as a child; exposed to illicit activity at an early age; diagnosed with a learning disorder; failed multiple grades; suspended an excessive number of times from school; dropped out of high school; became a teenage parent; and jailed at an early age. That may be where the statistical similarity ends, though. According to the psychological literature, the aforementioned circumstances disproportionately predispose adolescents to be abusers, to continue illicit behavior in adulthood, to have difficulty maintaining employment and, as a result, to remain poor and disenfranchised.

Craig J. Boykin is none of these things. In an inspirational display of faith and tenacity, Boykin refused to allow those circumstances to doom him to life in a perpetual loop of absentee fatherhood, involvement with the penal system, poverty, violence, and willful ignorance. In this book, he tells readers how he turned major obstacles into hurdles that strengthened and prepared him for a brighter future.

This book is a must-read for anyone interested in learning about and helping the beleaguered African American male. Readers will learn about Boykin's journey from blaming others to taking personal responsibility for his situation. In this book, Boykin draws the reader into the mindset of a proactive overcomer. Find out what this teenager said and did as he sat in jail as a result of his wife's and grandmother's statements against him! Find out what this Auburn University graduate said and did when his first college professor told him that he, "…wasn't college material…"! Find out what this injured veteran said and did as he was berated and belittled publicly by his disbelieving commanding officers! Boykin's experiences are excellent examples of self-confidence, self-control, and a drive to succeed. This book will not disappoint!

My Life, **DEDICATION**

This book is dedicated to my wife (Adrienne M. Boykin), I am a movement by myself, but together we're an unstoppable force. I would like to commend you for your continued support in all my endeavors.

This book is also dedicated to my grandparents (Alice & James Wright) for all the love and support they showed me throughout my life.

This book is dedicated to every person, young or old, employed or unemployed, educated or uneducated, that dreams of becoming something greater in life and desires to build a happy, successful, and rewarding life, but is too overwhelmed to take that first step. It is the hope and dream of Craig J. Boykin that this book might be that first step and inspire you to "Make Life Count" and become great.

This book is also dedicated to my daughter Kiera Boykin. I love you so very much.

This book is dedicated to my brother; keep your head up and continue to grow and move forward in life. I expect great things from you.

This book is dedicated to my real friends that have always been there for me in life: Lavon Lewis, Kendrick

Knox, DeAndre Caldwell, Rahiem Phifer, Jamaal Dingle, Sherrod Shackelford (Vik), Eddie Barnes, Ahmad Perry Sr., Christopher Lance Spears, Ethan Rozier and Nate Traywick (mentee).

This book is dedicated to my mother, simple put; I love you and always will!

This book is dedicated to that adjunct professor (can't remember her name) at Auburn University Montgomery who tutored me to the point that I could achieve all my goals.

To all of my extended family, friends, mentees, clients, colleagues, social media family, United Dream Montgomery members and anyone who has ever uttered a word of praise and/or prayed for me. I feel your prayers and I love and appreciate you all - this is for you!

My Life, **PREFACE**

There is no longer a need for predictions, hand-wringing, or apprehension about losing a generation of young people. It is severely too late. In education, employment readiness, economics, incarceration, health, housing, and parenting, we have lost a generation of young people. The only question that remains is, "Will we "America" lose the next two or three generations, or possibly every generation of blacks hereafter to the streets, negative media, gangs, drugs, poor education, unemployment, father absence, crime, violence, lack of parenting and death?"

The social and economic impacts on the Black communities of incarcerated Black males are enormous. The continuous exodus of young Black males from their communities to the prison systems destabilizes the family unit, and promotes an artificial scarcity of Black males that other than natural causes, further reduces the number of men available to women as possible marriage partners. As a result, this situation accelerates the propensity for the creation of fatherless, out-of-wedlock children with pent-up social and psychological scars with under-achievement as a birthright. The ex-felons from these Black communities also suffer from disenfranchisement policies that permanently strip them of their suffrage rights.

In this book, take a journey through the psyche of a true inspiration who overcame many of the same social and economic issues of those being shipped off to prison camps across America.

My Life, **INTRODUCTION**

How do you motivate someone to the point that they are able to transform the entire course of their life? Motivation is very important and the first step in motivating anyone is to understand the basic needs that drive motivation. For example, there is the need to succeed, the need to belong, the need for stimulation and excitement, the need for attention, power, and love.

Literacy levels amongst minorities are lower on average than they should be. Many scholars have written on the subject, attempting to find a reason for and a solution to the problem. There is some confusion over where the source of the problem lies. For example, some believe that an improvement in the curriculum will solve much of the problem.

However, the problem is more likely due to a lack of motivation amongst minority students to work hard in school. Engaging minorities so that they are interested in education is a daunting task, but it is an important issue that must be addressed. Achieving success outside of dangerous careers in organized crime is nearly impossible without a solid academic foundation.

Generational Ignorance is the worse,

because to the individuals who are exhibiting

the ignorance, in most cases they don't see

anything wrong with their actions, because these

actions have been integrated into their value

system as normal, because this is what they saw

or was taught as normal!

– Unknown Author

CHAPTER I
My Life, **Humble Beginnings**

CRAIG J. BOYKIN

MY LIFE, **YOUR**
INSPIRATION

**HOW TO TURN MINOR SETBACKS,
INTO A MAJOR COMEBACK!**

AN INSPIRATIONAL JOURNEY FROM GED TO PhD

Somewhere around 1978 my mother moved to Montgomery, Alabama after leaving her mother's house at an early age. Two years after my mother moved to Montgomery, Alabama, she encountered my father and shortly afterwards became impregnated by him. After discovering that she was pregnant, my mother informed him of her condition. Frightened and hesitant, as to what to do, my father, decided to abandon any responsibilities and he joined the U.S. Army.

Growing up with an absent parent can instill a deep sense of loss and shame in kids, especially when the absence appears to be voluntary. For some kids, abandonment extends beyond a parent's failure to support the child financially, and includes the failure to communicate with the child or play an active role in the child's life. Sadly, parental abandonment, and its effects, often leaves children with lingering questions about their own self-worth.

My mother did not tell anyone that she was pregnant. She went the entire nine months of her pregnancy without any prenatal care. The first time anyone knew that she was pregnant was when she went into labor with me. Even though she didn't receive any prenatal care I was born 7 pounds 6 ounces and healthy.

According to Eunice Kennedy Shriver National Institute of child health and human development, Women who suspect they may be pregnant should schedule a visit with their health care provider to begin prenatal care as soon as possible. Prenatal visits to a health care provider include a physical exam, weight checks, and providing a urine sample. Depending on the stage of the pregnancy, health care providers may also do blood tests and imaging tests, such as ultrasound exams. These visits also include discussions about the mother's health, the infant's health, and any questions about the pregnancy.

Preconception and prenatal care can help prevent complications and inform women about important steps they can take to protect their infant and ensure a healthy pregnancy. With regular prenatal care women can:

Reduce the risk of pregnancy complications. Following a healthy, safe diet; getting regular exercise as advised by a health care provider; and avoiding exposure to potentially harmful substances such as lead and radiation can help reduce the risk of problems during pregnancy and ensure the infant's health and development. [1]

Even though my mother didn't receive any prenatal care, I was fairly healthy as an infant, until I was about two years of age. At age two, I had to spend several weeks in the hospital with a severe case of pneumonia. My case was so severe that the doctors didn't believe that I would make it through the night.

---

1 http://houstonlifestyles.com/navigating-your-way-through-a-healthy-pregnancy/

My tongue had swollen so thick that I couldn't swallow. Fortunately, I pulled through and survived.

For the first part of my childhood, I lived with my grandmother. I would see my mother periodically here and there, but mostly she was nowhere to be found. When I was about 3 years old my mother married my stepfather. My mother would eventually become impregnated with her second child, my brother. Sometime after marrying my stepfather something happened that caused my eyes to become strabismus (being cross-eyed). It was said that I fell off the bed onto my head, but this was never confirmed. Unfortunately, my mother and my stepfather never truly admitted what really happened to me.

Strabismus (being cross-eyed) can be caused by problems with the eye muscles, the nerves that transmit information to the muscles, or the control center in the brain that directs eye movements. In theory, a hard blow to the head could make a person cross-eyed, but it is not very likely.[2]

My mother and stepfather would drink almost daily. And after a while, the drinking would turn into physical altercations between the two. As a young child, I witnessed my mother being beaten by my stepfather fairly often. One particular evening my stepfather, mother and a couple of their friends were playing cards, when I witnessed my

2 http://www.chacha.com/question/can-you-become-cross-eyed-by-hitting-your-head-really-hard

stepfather giving my younger brother a sip of alcohol from his cup. My stepfather continued to do this over and over until my younger brother eventually stumbled and passed out. I vividly remember images of all the adults in the room laughing as my brother would stagger and pass out on the floor.

My mother and stepfather began to fight very regularly. My mother was severely beaten almost daily. One evening during a vicious beating, my stepfather picked up my mother over his head and slammed her to the ground. During another vicious beating, my brother ran and picked up a knife and stabbed my stepfather in a feeble attempt to get him to stop beating our mother. Time went on, and the beatings continued and my mother eventually became pregnant with my younger sister. I guess by this time my mom had become weary and tired of taking those beatings. After my sister was born my mother and stepfather separated and eventually divorced.

What is very destructive psychologically for children is for them to experience their parents' continuing, unresolved, hostile conflicts. Research indicates that children are resilient and highly adaptive in general and can usually cope with and adapt to difficult situations such as separation and divorce. What severely damages children emotionally is bitter, long-lasting, ongoing conflict between parents, whether the parents live together or not.

The longer parental conflict continues and the greater the tension between the parents, the greater the likelihood that psychological difficulties will result for children such as emotional and behavior problems, anxiety, depression, sleep problems, low self-esteem, difficulties in school and a number of other difficulties. [3]

After my mother's divorce she started spending a lot of time with her then best friend, Faye. Faye had a younger daughter that was around the same age as I, named Lisa. Faye and her daughter Lisa would often come around. Lisa and I became very close friends.

Whenever my mother and Faye mother would go out drinking or partying they would always leave me and Lisa home along. It wasn't long before curiosity took over. I began to get curious about Lisa because she was a girl and I guess Lisa became curious about me because I was a boy. Neither one of our mothers really went out of their way to hide anything they engaged in with their male friends. Lisa and I began doing things that we saw our mothers doing. This went on for a number of years until one day when my mother was having a get together.

They were playing cards and drinking, as always. Lisa and I waited until all of the adults were in the house drinking and playing cards when we assembled as many trash cans

3 http://www.kathyeugster.com/articles/article002.htm

as possible and put them in a circle behind our apartment. Once the trash cans were in place, Lisa and I took off all our clothes and layed on top of one another. Lisa and I had no idea what it was that we were doing.

After about 15 minutes of engaging in these activities our parents came outside and caught us. Lisa's mother took her home. My mother brought me inside the house and took off all my clothes and put me in the bathtub.

Then my mother took me out of the bathtub and had her friends (who were all drunk) hold me down, while she beat me with an extension cord. The pain was so unbearable that I began to fight, twist, and turn trying to free my arms and legs. I eventually broke free but my mother continued swinging the extension cord and with one power swing she accidently hit me across my penis with the extension cord and blood splattered all over the walls, in the bed, and the floors. My mother was terrified; she immediately put me back in the bathtub, in an attempt to get the bleeding to stop. Eventually, the bleeding stopped, but I was never taken to the hospital for any type of evaluation.

Poverty affects the development and educational outcomes beginning in the earliest years of an individual's life, both directly and indirectly through mediated, moderated, and transactional processes. Educational readiness, or an individual's ability to use and profit from an education, has been recognized as playing a unique role in escaping from poverties grip in the United States. It is a critical element but needs to be supported by many other components of a poverty alleviation strategy, such as improved opportunity structures and empowerment of families. [4]

4 http://liferesolutionsaustralia.wordpress.com/2013/04/04/parental-conflict-how-it-can-be-harmful-for-children/

CHAPTER II
My Life, School Days

CRAIG J. BOYKIN

MY LIFE, YOUR
INSPIRATION

HOW TO TURN MINOR SETBACKS, INTO A MAJOR COMEBACK!

AN INSPIRATIONAL JOURNEY FROM GED TO PhD

The earliest grade I can remember is third. My brother and sister and I attended Forest Avenue Elementary School. Every day like clockwork, when we came home from school we would have to put down our belongings and go back to the school's park until the streetlights came on. I rarely remember ever doing any homework. If Forest Avenue had any issues they would reluctantly call my mother because she had a reputation for coming up there and cursing out the teachers and administrators.

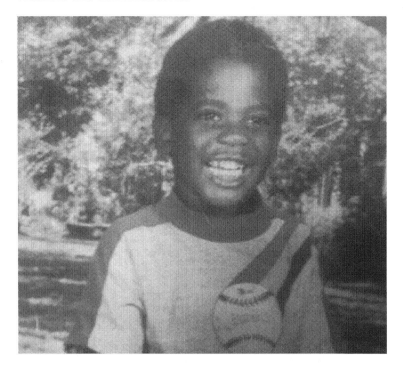

It took a while for me to fully understand why my mother would make us go to the park every day after school. The first time I realized my mom was doing drugs was when I came home one day and found her in the living room with a white couple that looked very similar to hippies. They wore bell bottoms and very bright clothes. They also had long hair as well.

Children who grow up in an environment of illicit drug use may first see their parents using drugs. This may put them at a higher risk for developing an addiction later in life for both environmental and genetic reasons. Alcoholism and other drug addictions tend to run in families. Children of addicted parents are more at risk for alcoholism and other drug abuse than are other children. [1]

My mother would often make us go in the back room and close all doors while she did her drugs. It seems like every day after we came home from school there would be different people at our house just hanging out. 1902 South Hall Street became the hang out spot for all the local dunks and addicts in the neighborhood. I would often find old medication bottles with holes punched in the side and foil covering the top.

Many people think that crack smells like plastic. Sometimes it may have no scent at all. Also, the smell can be attributed to the products the crack is cut with, such as baking soda or ether. [2]

---

1 http://www.nlm.nih.gov/medlineplus/ency/article/001522.htm
2 http://answers.ask.com/health/addictions/what_does_crack_smell_like

I would always take those "homemade crack pipes" and flush them down the toilet. Eventually my mother caught on to what I was doing and would beat me. My situation at home was extremely difficult. We stayed in a one bedroom shotgun home. For those who are unaware of what a shotgun house is; it is a house that you can stand at the front door and see the backdoor. A shotgun house typically has one room leading into the next without hallways. Shotgun architecture is now recognized as an African American contribution to American architectural styles.

As If the situation wasn't difficult enough there were countless times when we didn't have any food, running water, electricity, etc. The few times we did have food, if you were to open the refrigerator, roaches would scatter everywhere. Roaches were in our cabinets, beds, and even our clothes. One normal day at school I remember opening up my back pack and several roaches ran out. This was one of the most embarrassing moments of my childhood. The other kids joked and made fun of me the entire school year. The condition of the bathroom was so horrible that I hated to use the bathroom. This caused me to go weeks at a time without bathing. I didn't start brushing my teeth until I was 14.

One night around midnight there was a loud scream coming from the living room. I jumped out of bed along with my younger brother and ran to see what the commotion was. What we found was a man choking my mother with his knee in her chest, attempting to rip off her clothes. The man was attempting to rape my mother. I guess they had been drinking and doing drugs and he decided that he wanted to have sex with my mother, and she refused. My brother ran and grabbed a knife from the kitchen; I picked up a lamp off the table and threatened a man. He eventually left. That night was very difficult for me, I recall lying in bed shaking, still terrified by the events that had just transpired.

Another day for whatever reason, my brother, sister, and I woke up late and we didn't attend school. An unknown man came over and picked us up in his vehicle. My mother, sister, brother, Faye, and her daughter Lisa, and I all got in his car with him. My mother and Faye went into Burger King to get us some breakfast. As soon as they exited the vehicle, the strange man pulled out a pocket knife, turned around toward the back seat, where I was, and put the knife to my throat.

The man told me, with my brother, sister, and Lisa, all watching that "he would kill me, if I ever stayed my ass out of school again." No one in the car said anything; we rode around with that man all day. My mother didn't know what happened until we eventually arrived back home.

By this time, my mother's crack habits had begun to get worse. She would send me to the corner store with a one dollar food stamp (this was before EBT cards) and have me buy a 10 cent egg; receiving the change in coins. She would continue to send me to the store until she had enough change to buy her drugs.

One night my mother decided that she was going to go out to a club. After an unsuccessful attempt at finding someone to keep us, my mother decided to leave us at home alone with her friend named "Tag". Tag was someone we all knew; he would hang around, drink, smoke, and party with my mother. My mother came in and told me that Tag was going to be watching us tonight. My siblings and I got into the bed not thinking much about the situation. We could hear Tag and the other guys drinking and making a lot of commotion on the front porch as we lay in the bed. The next morning as we got up to get ready for school; my mother was nowhere to be found.

However, upon further review of the house, I began to notice that certain things were missing. The television was missing, the microwave, food out the refrigerator, the iron, and just random things throughout the house. Afraid and not knowing what to do, I helped my brother and sister put on their clothes and we walked to the gas station and called my grandmother. She eventually came and got us and took us to her house.

With all the chaos going on at home, it began to trickle over into my academics. My elementary school experience was very unpleasant, my eyes where crossed, and many times

I'd wear the same clothes two or three times a week. I rarely bathed and often went to school with a body odor. My grades began to slip in school. I was involved in a lot of altercations with other students. While I was in third grade the teachers and counselors became increasingly concerned about my behavioral actions and the lack of educational involvement. One report card I made all (F)'s, one in every subject. It was evident at this point that I had given up academically. The results of the learning disability examination stated that I had a learning disability. With this information the school informed my mother that they were placing me in a special education program. My brother would also go through the same process years later and be placed in special education with a learning disability.

Students, especially those attending high-poverty urban schools with student bodies primarily made up of minority students—continue to be the underperformers of the U.S. educational system. Many of these students fall far behind the achievement levels of their age mates in more advantaged U.S. neighborhoods or in other countries and begin showing clear signs of behavioral and emotional disengagement from school at early ages. [3]

I remember thinking that my life was over. I didn't want to be the student that everyone joked on and laughed at because I was dumb.

3 http://web.jhu.edu/sebin/q/b/PreventingStudentDisengagement.pdf

Special education and students with learning disabilities are often deemed as stupid by their peers. Unfortunately, I ended up repeating the third and fifth grade. I wasn't able to overcome my circumstances. I would get suspended from school almost monthly for various incidents. The situation became so bad that they would send me home during the middle of the day. This is against all rules and regulations because the school was still accountable for me and if something would have happened to me walking home they would have been liable. In most cases when I was suspended from school and walked home my mother would still be in the bed. Either she would tell me to go in my room or I would have to sit in the back yard until my siblings got home from school.

African American males challenge educators in many ways. Perhaps the single most important challenge that has garnered recent attention in research reports, policy documents, and public commentary has been the increasing disparity in the educational achievement of African American males relative to their peers. Although other issues, such as the need to develop programs that promote school readiness, improving teacher education, and providing resources to meet increasing academic standards, are important, the implications for achievement differentials are even more far-reaching.

The negative consequences of the achievement gap are more acute for African American males who are victimized by chronic, systemic levels of poor performance and behavior problems in school. In short, the potential loss of resources— intellectual, cultural, and economic—resulting from lower achievement reduces the capacity of African American males to be productive, integral, and contributing members of their communities. [4]

One day, I remember walking around the house and seeing something on the living room floor that looked similar to a balloon. So I picked it up and I began popping it. My mother screamed at me to put it in the trash and to go wash my hands. I later came to the understanding that what I was playing with was a used condom.

The summer before my sixth grade year, I was playing with some fireworks that I found at my grandmother's house and I accidentally set an entire field on fire. The police and fire department came and put the fire out. I was terrified that I was going to jail but all they did was take my name down and tell me that I wasn't allowed to play with any form of fireworks ever again.

That same summer, I guess my brother had gotten into my grandmother's firearms. One day while I was laying on the coach watching television, my brother came in the room with what seemed to be a toy hand gun. He pointed the hand gun at my head like he had seen on TV, then he put it to my head;

4 http://uex.sagepub.com/content/38/5/515.abstract

I didn't think anything of it because I thought it wasn't real. He was just about to pull the trigger until my grandmother came in and took the gun away from him and told him that it wasn't anything to play with and to never touch it again.

The new school year would bring excitement to me because I was one year away from middle school. In sixth grade, I meet Ms. Gaston. I was so excited about sixth grade because I really wanted to play sports in middle school. I was already two years older than most of my classmates. Ms. Gaston would put my desk next to her desk often. Ms. Gaston was the first person that ever held me accountable or made me feel like I was special. One afternoon while we were playing at the park after school, it started raining very badly. As we started walking home, Ms. Gaston pulled up and gave us a ride home.

The last day of my sixth grade year I remember Ms. Gaston telling me that she believed in me, and that my situation did not have to dictate my future. Ms. Gaston told me that "either you will work hard now (in school) or you will have work hard for the rest your life Craig." This was the first time in my life that I truly felt special.

By the time I made it to junior high school things had begun to get a little better. My mom met a really nice guy. They would eventually get married and he would become my stepfather. In middle school I played football and basketball and was pretty good at it. Sports gave me an outlet. It also was the motivation that I needed to stay out of trouble. One day during my ninth grade school year my brother who was in the seventh grade; I remember it like it was yesterday because I often ask myself what if I would have given my brother the keys to my car.

My brother approached me one morning and asked me if he could see the keys to my car, (I was driving a car to school in the 9th grade); for whatever reason I told my brother no. I remember the look in my brother's eyes after I replied no; it was as if I had just sentenced him to death. Around fourth period the same day, I was eating lunch in the lunch room when someone came and told me that my brother was in the office getting arrested.

After franticly running to the office, I finally found out what had happened. My brother had taken my grandmother's handgun from her house and given it to his friend. A couple of days later, his friend brought the pistol back to school and gave it back to my brother, and this is when all hell broke loose.

That day, the police took my brother and his friend to the department of youth services. My brother was kicked out of the Montgomery Public Schools at age 13 and could not return. This was the first time he was incarcerated, but it wouldn't be his last. Kicked out of school and nothing to do, my brother started getting into major trouble. My brother began engaging in gang activity and associating with some very negative individuals. He was in and out of boot camps for various reasons. He started stealing, robbing and selling drugs. He ultimately went to prison when he was 17, got out at 20 and went back within six months for seven more years.

A black male born in 1991 has a 29% chance of spending time in prison at some point in his life. Nearly one in three African American males aged 20–29 are under some form of criminal justice supervision whether imprisoned, jailed, on parole or probation. One out of nine African American men will be incarcerated between the ages of 20 and 34. Black males ages 30 to 34 have the highest incarceration rate of any race/ethnicity.[5]

During my middle school years I was an athlete determined and driven to succeed. This motivated me not to get into trouble, and although I was in special education I passed all my classes. In ninth grade my football team won the city championship and I was voted All-City (which means I was one of the best at my position in the city of Montgomery). My basketball team was very successful that year as well. After basketball season was over I received a phone call from the head basketball coach at Catholic High School here in Montgomery, Alabama.

---

5 *http://en.wikipedia.org/wiki/Statistics_of_incarcerated_African-American_males*

The coach came to my house and met with my mother and told her that he wanted to give me a scholarship to come and play basketball for him at Catholic.

I started dating a young lady during the summer before my freshmen year at Catholic High. No one in my family, nor was any of my friends too fond of this young lady. One day during the summer when I was at her house a young man came to the door and he asked to speak with her. When she want outside I went behind her and I remember the guy had a bandanna tied around his head like Tupac would wear.

After a brief altercation between him and I, he pulled out a gun and pointed it at me. At that point, I told him it wasn't that serious and left. My best friend attended the same school as the young lady and he would always tell me that he never really trusted her and that she had a very bad reputation at their school for sleeping with a lot of guys. A few months after the situation the young lady told me that she was pregnant. Concerned and frightened, I didn't know what to do, because I felt like I was replicating the cycle of my mother and father. After telling my mother and seeing her disappointment, I did the notable thing and began to do what I could to help her with the situation that we had created. I would leave school early to take her to doctor appointments. I started saving money because I knew the baby would need clothes and other baby items.

This continued until one day when her sister came to me and told that the baby wasn't mine. I questioned my girlfriend about the baby not being mine and she broke down and started crying, telling me that the guy that pulled the gun on me that day had raped her. I never truly believed her because her sister had already told me that they were messing around behind my back. However, she was willing to lie to the fullest extent. She wanted me to take her to the police station so she could press charges. I knew immediately that the guy didn't rape her and I wasn't willing to have a bogus rape charge put against him for something I know he didn't do. That day I got in my car and left never to return.

With all that was going on, I was somehow able to get myself together and get ready for my freshman year in high school and the up and coming basketball season. By this time I was staying with my grandmother because my mother kicked me out the house. One night while I was on the phone with my girlfriend, my stepfather asked me to get off the phone and I refused. We were in involved in a physical altercation which lead to my mother kicking me and my younger brother out the house.

Only 3 out of 100 Black males entering kindergarten will graduate from college. Every 5 seconds during the school day, a Black public school student is suspended. Every 46 seconds during the school day, a Black high school student drops out. Every minute, a Black child is arrested and a

Black baby is born to an unmarried mother. Every 3 minutes, a Black child is born into poverty. Every hour, a Black baby dies. Every 4 hours, a Black child or youth under 20 dies from an accident, and every 5 hours, a Black youth is a homicide victim. Every day, a Black young person under 25 dies from HIV infection and a Black child or youth under 20 commits suicide. [6]

My first day at Catholic high was a very different experience. One of the first things that I noticed was there were only about ten black students out of 400. And out of these ten black students eight were athletes. Another thing that was different was the fact that it was a private Catholic school. Some of the white students at the school tried to make my academic life very difficult. My grandmother didn't have a lot of money so there were days when I would have to steal biscuits and chicken sandwiches during breakfast and lunch from the school cafeteria. The irony is that the lunch room workers were fully aware of what I was doing, although they never said anything to me.

One of the most difficult things about this new school was the academics. Coming from public school with a learning disability and having repeated two grades, I was probably reading on a fifth grade level. Catholic High School did something different. If you were an athlete it was mandatory that you stay 30 minutes after school.

_6 http://blackeducator.blogspot.com/2008_02_01_archive.html_

The 30-minute tutoring was called tutorials. My teachers went out of their way to work with me and try to bring me up to speed with the other students. This is when they found out that I couldn't even write a five sentence paragraph.

My basketball team had a very successful season. The season before I came to Catholic high, they were 2-22, my first season we went 18-12. After basketball season was over, I was paged to the office, because the principal needed to speak with me. After speaking with the principal he informed me that I couldn't come back to school until I brought my grandmother with me. The next day after waiting a while, he finally called us in. Initially the conversation started with him stating that I haven't paid tuition the entire school year.

It was my understanding that I didn't have to pay any tuition. It was made very clear from the first day that my family couldn't afford to pay any money for me to attend a private school. To make matters worse, this was the first time all year that I was informed that I needed to pay something. The principal informed me and my grandmother that I could no longer attend Catholic High School. The principal also stated that a complaint from one of the caucasian female students said that I had inappropriately said something to her and her father wanted me put in jail, but they decided to kick me out of school instead.

This is the same young lady in which I had many altercations with her boyfriend throughout the school year. Nevertheless the principal gave me my transcriptions and told me that the best thing would be for me to go and enroll in another high school. Sixteen and reading on a 5th grade school level; I didn't have the motivation to go enroll in another high school and try to get caught up. I made an executive decision to just forgo any more schooling and I dropped out.

A 2006 study by The Manhattan Institute surveyed 100 of the largest school districts in the United States and found that only 48 percent of African-American males earned a diploma—that's 11 percent less than African-American females. More troubling is the research that shows on an average day, one and four Black males who drop out of high school will end up incarcerated. High rates of placement in special education classes and disproportionate use of suspension and expulsion only exacerbate the problem. The graduation numbers for Black males are dismal, chilling, and undeniably pathetic. The nation graduates only 47% of Black males who enter the 9th grade. Black males face an upheaval educational battle: their graduation statistics are sobering across America. My grandmother pleaded with me on several attempts to go back to school but I just didn't feel that there was any hope in me going back. When I told my mother that I had dropped out she just looked at me and didn't have any comments. [7] Today's young people are

7 http://www.bet.com/news/national/2011/08/16/why-are-more-black-males-dropping-out-of-high-school.html

partners, parents, workers, citizens of tomorrow. Unless they master the skills required to manage their own emotions, treat others with respect, negotiate points of disagreement and conflict, build their capacity for productive work, and work cooperatively with others, America's society as a whole will suffer.[8]

It is amazing how growing up poor in the ghetto brings out the best in some individuals and the worse in other individuals!

- Unknown Author

8 http://www.aracy.org.au/publications-resources/command/download_file/id/122/file-name/Preventing_Youth_Violence_-_What_does_and_doesn%27t_work_and_why.pdf

CHAPTER III
My Life, **Rock Bottom**

CRAIG J. BOYKIN

MY LIFE, **YOUR**
INSPIRATION

HOW TO TURN MINOR SETBACKS, INTO A MAJOR COMEBACK!

AN INSPIRATIONAL JOURNEY FROM GED TO PhD

Shortly after dropping out of high school I meet another young lady that I started dating. She also dropped out of high school and became a mother at the age of 14. She had been kicked out of her mother's house at early age. She had also been introduced to stripping by a friend. Not long after, we moved in together. Her mother helped us get a two bed room apartment. Around the same time she received a large sum of money that her father had put up for her. So at this point I was eighteen and an instant father to her three-year-old daughter.

Things went pretty smoothly until the money ran out. Neither one of us worked the entire time we were blowing the money. But like the old saying, "all good things must come to an end" and when the money ran out, the situation became really uncomfortable. Neither she nor I finished school so looking for employment was very difficult seeing that we also had no work experience.

One time when we were renting an apartment and instead of paying the power bill, I took the power bill money and rented a big screen TV from Rent a Center. The same day that it was supposed to be delivered, I received a knock at the door, I ran to the door thinking it was my new big screen TV, but it was actually the power company disconnecting my power; then 30 minutes later the TV arrived. I sat in the living room just looking at the TV for hours with no power, many hot, sticky powerless nights later, I finally got up enough money to pay the power bill and the power was turned back on. However, by that time, the TV was picked up by Rent a Center the day before, and I never once had an opportunity to even see how the TV looked plugged in!

Researchers offer a few theories on why so many individuals have gone broke after receiving large sums of money. Prior research has shown that if individuals have below-average incomes and education; it's no great leap to assume they tend to have limited financial literacy (even compared with a general population that has been shown to sorely lack it). Individuals who receive large lump sums might also engage in something behavioral economists call mental accounting by treating their new money less cautiously than they would their normal earnings. [1]

One night around 9 pm, I received a phone call from my brother asking me to come and pick him up from the bowling alley. This wasn't unusual, because my brother would always ask me to come and pick him up. Upon arriving at the bowling alley, I witnessed my brother and another young man in an intense altercation. After several verbal exchanges back and forth, my brother and his friends got into my car. I asked my brother what's the problem, and he stated that the dude was a fu*king slob. A slob is an insult or a derogatory term to Blood's gang members to mean 'put down'.

---

1 http://terra-biotech.blogspot.com/2012/09/lottery-me-not-nectr-me-lots.html

The Bloods is a street gang founded in Los Angeles and is widely known for its rivalry with other gang. [2]

Prior to pulling off, the guy called my brother a fu*king donut, which was a derogatory term for the black gangster disciples (my brother's gang). In most cases, these derogatory terms would get an individual killed in the streets. Nevertheless, I pulled out of the bowling alley parking lot and proceeded down the eastern boulevard. As I turned onto the bypass, another car speeded pass me and opened fire on my truck. Unbeknownst to anyone in the car, the guy my brother just had the altercation with, pulled out of the parking lot behind us in his car. I have watched countless movies and real life gun shots sound nothing like the movies. The shots sounded like something zipping really fast past my ear. It took me a minute to realize what was taking place.

When I came to myself, I realized that the individual in the back seat had been shot in the head. So, I franticly rushed him to the hospital while calling 911 on my cell phone. Once I arrived at the hospital we pulled him out of the back seat and rushed him into the emergency room. The nurses begin to question us as to what just transpired. As I began explaining, I was interrupted by a loud "oh my God" your arm bleeding. The nurse was referring to me. I had been shot and didn't even know it. I assume that my adrenaline was rushing so fast and I didn't even feel the bullet piercing my flesh.

---

2 http://www.ask.com/question/what-is-a-gang-slob

By this time, the police arrived at the hospital. They begin searching my vehicle for weapons. The police insistently asked my brother and his friend "where are the guns" over and over. They took my brother and his friend to the police station for questioning while I and the other young man received medical treatment.

Eventually we both landed a job working at Subway making minimum wage and barely making enough money to pay rent and bills. The arguments and physical altercations became more common and more intense. Doing the time, I was working at subway I opened up a checking account with a local bank. Clueless as to how a checking account works I begin writing checks all over Montgomery. Every day I would write checks just so we could have something to eat, pay bills, rent, get gas, buy clothes, etc.

Not long after the shooting, I received a letter in the mail from the District Attorney's office stating that I had several bounced checks in their office and I needed to come to the listed address as soon as possible. Frighten and concerned, I went right down to the DA's office and they placed me on a payment plan.

Eventually, we were evicted from our apartment and she moved back home with her mother and I moved back in with my grandmother. While staying at home with my grandmother I wasn't working. So I would go in my grandmother's purse, and steal any cash that she had and take her checks, make them out to myself, take them to the bank and cash them. It had gotten so bad, to the point where I was taking money from her every day. I guess my grandmother became wise that someone was writing her checks. So she went to the bank and had an alert placed on her account.

One day, after stealing one of my grandmother's checks, I went to the bank to cash the $40 dollar check I wrote to myself. All while not knowing that my grandmother had placed an alert on the account; they called her and she told them that she had not given me permission and not to cash the check. I really did not know the severity of what I was doing when I was bouncing all these checks or stealing money from my grandmother.

I was on my way home from dropping my grandmother off at church when I was pulled over by a sheriff of Montgomery County. When the sheriff pulled me over he asked me for my driver's license, insurance, and registration. I really wasn't nervous because I had never been in trouble with the law before and as far as I knew my license was valid.

Little did I know that when my grandmother called the police about someone stealing and writing her checks, this same sheriff came out and ran the social security number and date of birth on the check. This wasn't the first time I had been pulled over by the police and I really didn't think anything of it. When the sheriff came back to the car, he politely asked me to step out of the vehicle.

I thought that it was rather peculiar that I had to step out of the vehicle. He asked me to put my hands on the top of the car. Then he informed me that I had two warrants for my arrest and a hold by the city of Montgomery; so I immediately tensed up and the sheriff could tell and he reacted aggressively (not overly aggressively) but enough to counteract my fear.

At this point, I asked the sheriff could I take my grandmother's car to the house because we were minutes away from her house. The officer handcuffed me to the steering wheel of the car. After dropping the car off with my grandfather, I was taken to the county jail. During in-processing they informed me that I had a warrant for harassment, one for forged instrument (checks), and three outstanding traffic tickets with the city of Montgomery and there was a hold placed on me. Meaning when I bonded out of the county jail, they would release me over to the city jail and I would have to see a judge before I could be released.

To my surprise the harassment warrant was signed by my girlfriend. The forged instrument warrant (checks) was signed by my grandmother. At this this point, I became really furious, because the harassment warrant was fabricated by my girlfriend. She and I had many altercations but I never did what she stated I did in the warrant. As for the forged instrument, I deserved everything that could happen to me.

This happened early one Sunday morning so therefore I had to sit in jail all day until the next morning. The first night you are in a cell by yourself and I remember sitting in the jail cell that night thinking to myself that if I don't do something different with my life, it's going to continue to spiral out of control. The one thing in life I didn't want was to end up like my mother. So I made a decision, a vow, to myself that night when I get out of jail I was going to seek out something different. I prayed to God and ask Him for direction and guidance because I didn't want this to be my life.

That seemed to be the longest night ever. The next morning as I'm sitting, waiting on the guards to call us to go to court I was eating breakfast and talking with some of the others inmates. One of the inmates asked another, what he was in for and he said murder and the other said armed robbery, at that point, the seriousness of the situation became real to me. Finally, they called me into court. I saw the court appointed attorney for all about five minutes and he told me to plead guilty and I would most likely receive probation. Being young and naïve I went along with it as long as I didn't have to go to jail. The judge was going to send me to boot camp for six months; and when I noticed that the lawyer wasn't going to say anything further and just let me go to jail, I spoke up.

I told the judge that I just started working a new job and had a new born daughter and please don't lock me up. After a few seconds of pondering the judge recanted his decision and placed me on probation for the harassment charge, for the forged instrument he placed me on probation and I had to pay back my grandmother.

The biggest drawback to plea bargaining is for the innocent defendant who decides to plead guilty to a lesser charge in order to avoid the risk that he or she will be found guilty at trial. Additionally, some attorneys and judges argue that plea bargaining has led to poor police investigations and attorneys who do not take the time to properly prepare their cases.

They believe that instead of pursuing justice, the parties rely on making a deal and that the details of what happened and the legal consequences for those actions are less important. Some attorneys and judges also argue that plea bargaining is unconstitutional because it takes away a defendant's constitutional right to a trial by jury. If the defendant is coerced or pressured into a plea bargain agreement then this argument may have weight. [3]

After I got out of jail, I began almost immediately looking for a means out of this situation. Sitting home one day, I picked up the phone and I called the local job corps recruitment center. I set up an appointment with the job corps advisor.

3 *http://resources.lawinfo.com/en/articles/plea-bargaining-and-deals/federal/the-pros-and-cons-of-plea-bargaining.html*

The next day, I went down to the local job corps office. After a few preliminary questions she asked me when I could leave for Kentucky. I told her that I wanted to leave immediately.

She expressed to me that there was a process that I had to go through and I couldn't leave immediately, but I could leave within the next week or so. This worked out great because I had to get my situation straight with the courts of Montgomery. The first thing I did was I went back to court even though I wasn't on the docket for that court date. I sat the entire day in court until it ended then I asked for an opportunity to speak with the judge.

When given the opportunity, I explained to the judge that I was on probation for a harassment charge and was mandated to attend anger management classes. I also expressed to the judge that I was on probation for forged instrument but I had an opportunity to better myself by going to job corps.

The judge was very excited so much to the point that he suspended all my charges pending completion of the job corps program. So with that monkey off my back, now I was free to go to job corps and begin the process of a real-life change. All I had to do was report back to the court when I completed job corps. So, I packed up my belongings and loaded a plane and I was off to Carl D. Perkins Job Corps, in Prestonsburg, Kentucky.

Most people believe that complaining is the solution to their problem!

- Unknown Author

CHAPTER IV
My, Life, the Transition

CRAIG J. BOYKIN

MY LIFE, **YOUR**
INSPIRATION

HOW TO TURN MINOR SETBACKS, INTO A MAJOR COMEBACK!

AN INSPIRATIONAL JOURNEY FROM GED TO PhD

Job Corps is a free education and training program that helps young people learn skills for a career, earn a high school diploma or GED, and find and keep a good job. For eligible young people at least 16 years of age that qualify as low income, Job Corps provides the all-around skills needed to succeed in a career and in life. Job Corps provides an initial health checkup upon arrival at the center as well as basic health and medical services including dental and eye care. Job Corps is primarily a residential program, providing students with room, board and spending money while they learn. Twice a year, students are provided with paid vacations for home visits. [1]

Carl D. Perkins is a job corps center located in Prestonsburg, Kentucky. The center is one of the smaller job corps in the United States. The center consists of about 300 students. The job corps center picked us up from the airport and transported us to the center. The first week we were in orientation with OIP brothers and sisters. At the end of orientation we were assigned dorm rooms.

Each room is set up where it has three or four students per room with a room captain. Job corps was very different for me because they had a lot of rules and regulations in place to help students succeed. A lot of the students that went to job corps came from very dysfunctional and non-disciplined situations. The typical day for a job corps student started

---

1 http://www.jobcorps.gov/home.aspx

about 6:00 a.m. RA's or residential advisors would come through and wake us up. Between 6:00 and 7:00 am students were to shower, get dressed, make up their beds, clean up their room, and eat breakfast.

Job Corps has two main functions. Students can receive a trade and their GED. The student's day at Job Corps is broken up into two parts. The first part of the day focuses on your GED, the second half of the day focuses on the student's trade. Students that already have their GED or high school diploma would stay in their trade all day. [2]

The mission of the Job Corps program is to help economically challenged young adults become responsible, employable and productive citizens by providing them with opportunities to develop the vocational, educational and social skills needed to succeed. [3]

I selected retail sales as my trade because I always had a desire to work as an office manager. Students at Job Corps received a paycheck every two weeks. The allowance allowed students to buy personal items that they needed while they were attending Job Corps. To keep students entertained during down time, Job Corps supplied students with pool tables, a gym for basketball, weight room, theater, and various other forms of entertainment.

---

2 *http://www.jobcorps.gov/home.aspx*
3 *http://www.jobcorps.gov/home.aspx*

Although Job Corps had rules and regulations in place to help students succeed, many students were either kicked out or they dropped out of the program. Numerous female students left Job Corps pregnant. Many students would drink and smoke weed during the weekend and during the evenings after school. This wasn't really a temptation for me because I have never smoked weed or drank, because I associated that with being like my mother. Students who got caught fighting were sent home.

Statistics show that 80% of Job Corps graduates are placed in jobs, enrolled in full-time education or join the military.[4] Many of the students were just not used to the structure. Job Corps had many of the same roadblocks that you would face in the real world. For instance, you could buy marijuana, alcohol, cigarettes, Black & Mild cigars, food, snacks, etc.

In 1995, Job Corps instituted a zero tolerance policy for drugs and violence. Before entering the program, students must sign a contract committing to abide by the zero tolerance policy and stating that they are entering the program drug free. All students are tested for drugs upon entering Job Corps. Throughout their enrollment in Job Corps, students can be tested at any time if suspected of drug use. Any violent act is grounds for immediate expulsion. [5]

4 http://www.jobcorps.gov/home.aspx
5 http://www.jobcorps.gov/home.aspx

During my time at Job Corps I met a young lady that I started dating. She was two months pregnant when I arrived. She was pregnant by a young man who was previously kicked out of the program. The young lady was originally from Boston, Massachusetts but was enrolled in the Job Corps program from Alabama while living with her father. She left Job Corps not long after I got there due to her condition.

Pregnant females are not allowed to enroll in the program, and very few females become pregnant while in the program, but if they do they must leave once they reach a certain point. [6]

Job Corps had a basketball team that traveled to other centers to play competitive games. Being that I love basketball, I joined the team and would eventually become the captain. My stay a Job Corps over the course of a year was very smooth. I didn't have many altercations because I eventually became one of the leaders on campus.

I completed my trade in retail sales within six months. At that point I was studying for my GED full-time. After completing all my prerequisites, I was now in a position to go and take my GED test. I was really excited because earning my GED would give me an opportunity to begin succeeding in life and become a better person.

---

6 http://www.jobcorps.gov/home.aspx

The day was finally here, the van was coming to take me to the college where all Job Corps students took their GED test. I had a lot of trouble sleeping the night before. The morning of, I couldn't eat any breakfast; it felt like I had butterflies in my stomach. On this particular day, I was the only one taking the GED test.

When I got to the college, the Job Corps' representative gave me a number to call when I finished my test. The lady came into the room and she began to read the instructions and the procedures for the exam. About halfway through the exam I began to feel really sick. It literally felt like I had to vomit. I guess my nerves and the magnitude of the moment got the best of me, because that's exactly what I did, vomited all over the floor and table. The instructor came in and made sure I was ok and stopped the time. She had someone come in and clean up the vomit and I restarted the test.

I finished the test without any more incidents. Now the waiting game begins. I headed back to Job Corps and waited for my results. I was done with my trade and I was done with my GED. While I was waiting on my results I remembered one day seeing a flyer on the wall stating that the military recruiters were coming to our Job Corps Center.

Bored and having no interest in the Army, I decided to attend the recruiting fair. I didn't know what my next move would be, but I knew I didn't want to go back to Montgomery,

Alabama with just a diploma and a GED. I didn't feel like I would have the tools that I needed to become successful.

I attended the military recruiting fair and the recruiter speech was very inspiring to me, so much to the point that I decided to at least take the Armed Services Vocational Aptitude Battery (ASVAB) test and see what happens. A couple of days later I received my results. I had a very low score but the recruiter did inform me that he could still get me in with some provisions.

The ASVAB was first introduced in 1968 and was adopted by all branches of the military in 1976. In 2002 it underwent a major revision. In 2004, the test's percentile ranking scoring system was re-normalized, to ensure that a score of 50% really did represent doing better than exactly 50% of test-takers. The ASVAB currently contains 9 sections. The duration of each test varies from as low as ten minutes up to 36 minutes for Arithmetic Reasoning; the entire ASVAB is three hours long. [7]

The process of waiting on my GED results seem like it was taking forever. Therefore, I decided to go ahead and go back to Montgomery. Job Corps purchased me an airline ticket and I was on my way back home. When I got back to Montgomery, I went to live with my job corps girlfriend.

---

7 *https://en.wikipedia.org/wiki/Armed_Services_Vocational_Aptitude_Battery*

She lived in Monroeville which was about 40 to 50 miles from Montgomery.

One week after moving in with her, I received my results from my GED test. I passed all parts except one the language and writing section. Discouraged, I really didn't know what to do because I felt like I had let myself down and I didn't complete my goal. Not much longer after that things with the young lady and I didn't work out and I moved back to Montgomery to live with my grandmother.

I remember sitting on the bed going through a box of things from Job Corps thinking what am I going to do now when I ran across the recruiter's business card. So I called the recruiter and told him that I really wanted to go to the military now. The recruiter asked me how serious was I and I explained to him that I was very serious. The recruiter gave me a date and told me that he would drive down from Kentucky to pick me up.

During the meantime, I went back to court as ordered by the Judge. I informed the Judge that I completed Job Crops and had also enrolled in the military and was set to enlist in a week. The Judge congratulated me and said that he was proud of the effort I was making to turn my life around. He also stated that he was confident that basic training in the Army would get me to where I needed to be in life. Then he gave me youthful offender on the forged instrument charge and dismissed the harassment charge. I also went to the

Montgomery municipal court house and paid $1700.00 for unpaid traffic tickets that where currently warrants.

Youthful offender is a special status that not only limits the length of punishment and length of probation but greatly restricts the release of information to the general public. The law that determines Youthful Offender (YO) status is found in Section15-19-7, Code of Alabama (1975). It reads in pertinent part, "No determination made under the provisions of this chapter shall disqualify any youth for public office or public employment, operate as a forfeiture of any right or privilege or make him ineligible to receive any license granted by public authority, and such determination shall be deemed a conviction of a crime; provided, however, that he or she is not subsequently convicted of a crime, the prior adjudication shall be considered."

The Youthful Offender Act (was) intended to extricate persons below the age of twenty-one years of age from the harshness of criminal prosecution and conviction. It (was) designed to provide them with the benefits of an informal, confidential, rehabilitative system. Youthful Offender Proceedings are not criminal in nature. Youthful Offender adjudications are special proceedings designed to protect persons in a certain age group, heretofore tried as adults from the stigma and often harmful consequences of the criminal adjudicatory process. It is a manifestation of the legislature's judgment that while persons are still young may more readily and appropriately respond to methods of treatment which are more rehabilitative and more correctional and less severe than penalties to which adults are exposed. It is an extension, so to speak, of the protective juvenile process. The institution of special procedures is a right vested by the State and their application lies within the discretion of the State. [8]

The Army recruiter was well aware that I didn't finish my GED; however, he was able to pull some strings and still get me in. My ASVAB scores were so low, that I wasn't able to select a Military Occupational Specialties (MOS). The recruiter told me that every week during Basic Training I would be pulled out of training and go to classes that would train me on the ASVAB and I would have the opportunity to retake the test and raise my score so I can select a better military career.

8 http://wbarryalvislaw.com/Youthful_Offender_Status.html

CHAPTER V
My Life, the Solider

CRAIG J. BOYKIN

MY LIFE, **YOUR**
INSPIRATION

HOW TO TURN MINOR SETBACKS, INTO A MAJOR COMEBACK!

AN INSPIRATIONAL JOURNEY FROM GED TO PhD

I went through in-processing at Maxwell AFB (MEPS). MEPS is the Military Entrance Processing Station and it's no understatement to say that pretty much everything a person wants to do in the United States Military starts at the MEPS. MEPS would determine whether I meet the physical, mental and moral standards (as established by each branch of the Armed Forces) and decides whether the military and I will make a good fit. MEPS consisted of a lot of poking and being prodded and asked a lot of questions and asked to sign a lot of paperwork, and do a lot of waiting.

That morning my day started around 6:45 a.m. The first test I took was a blood pressure check and they checked my heart rate. Next they evaluated all my paperwork and ask me to verify that the information was accurate. Then they printed out barcodes and put them on folders and directed me to the hearing and vision testing. The first test is for color blindness I had to state what number I recognized in the colors. This is when I found out that I was color blind.

I had to take a vision, hearing, urine and blood test and breathalyzer test also. At this point they got my height and weight measured. Then a doctor gave me a physical exam. He asked me questions about my medical history, marijuana and alcohol usage. Then I did my Oath of Enlistment and was officially set to start my journey.

My first step would be Basic Training. I was assigned to Fort Benning, which is a United States Army post outside Columbus, Georgia that supports more than 120,000 active-duty military, family members, reserve component soldiers, retirees, and civilian employees on a daily basis. Basic Training is divided into two parts: Basic Combat Training and Advanced Individual Training.

Basic Combat Training (BCT) consists of the first ten weeks of the total Basic Training period, and is identical for all Army, Army Reserve, and Army National Guard recruits. This is where individuals learn about the fundamentals of being a soldier, from combat techniques to the proper way to address a superior. BCT is also where individuals undergo rigorous physical training to prepare their bodies and their minds for the eventual physical and mental strain of combat. One of the most difficult and essential lessons learned in BCT is self-discipline, as it introduces prospective soldiers to a strict daily schedule that entails many duties and high expectations for which most civilians are not immediately ready.[1]

The first place they sent me was the new recruit processing center. They directed me and others to our temporary barracks. I remember sitting in a chair while the Drill Sergeants were watching the NBA finals between the Indiana Pacers and the Los Angeles Lakers. After a full day of being issued all

1 http://www.forumforpages.com/facebook/ms-abct/army-basic-combat-training-bct-information/3856319183/0

our equipment and supplies we ate dinner and were sent to our barracks and instructed to get a good night rest, because we had to be up at four o'clock in the morning to start PT (physical training).

All the new recruits entered the barracks and put their things away and got ready for the next day. Lying in bed, I was excited and nervous at the same time. Eventually I fell asleep, and it seemed like not minutes after falling asleep, the Drill Sergeants came bursting in hollering and screaming for us to get up and get dressed. It was 3:30 in the morning. I don't think I have ever in my life been up so early. Rushing to get dress I put on my PT uniform and went outside. The Drill Sergeants put us into what is called a formation and we began to do push-ups, sit-ups, jumping jacks, and various other exercises for about an hour. Afterwards we went back in and took a shower and got dressed and ready for the day.

Drill Sergeants are the instructors that are responsible for most of the training that takes place in Basic Training. They accompany recruits throughout the training process, instructing and correcting them in everything from firing weapons to the correct way to address a superior, and are also largely responsible for the safety of recruits. They are recognizable by their distinctive headgear, often called "Smokey the Bear" hats, as they resemble that character's round park ranger-style hat. [2]

2 http://en.wikipedia.org/wiki/United_States_Army_Basic_Training

We did PT every day. This was getting us ready for the real training that would yet to come; this was just the processing center. After two weeks of being at the in-processing center the Drill Sergeants came and picked us up. The Drill Sergeants showed up with a school bus and we all got excited because the camp was miles away and were told that we would have to walk.

Seconds after the bus pulled up, countless Drill Sergeants came running off the bus screaming and yelling and we went running like chickens with our heads cut off.

They walked us to the bus and instructed us to place our belongings on the bus and line back up outside of the bus because we would be walking the five miles. This deflated our egos. The bags were riding the air conditioned bus and we had to walk five miles with an 80-pound duffle bag.

After a long exhausting road march to camp, we finally arrived. Once there the Drill Sergeants made us stand there for about an hour, motionless. We were so terrified that I don't even think we blinked, let alone moved. The Drill Sergeants gave us instructions on what would happen over the next 60 days during training.

Night one, the Drill Sergeants made all sixty-three soldiers, including myself, strip down to nothing and stand in a line heel to toe. This went on for about two hours before making us shower and hit the bed. That night I had the first shift of fireguard watch. Every night, at least two recruits from the platoon must be awake at any given time, patrolling their barracks area, watching for fires, cleaning the barracks, and watching for recruits attempting to leave the barracks area. They wake the next pair of recruits at the end of their two-hour shift. This duty is called fire guard.

Fire guard stems back to the days of wooden barracks and wood-burning stoves. The fire guard would watch the stoves to make sure that the barracks would not catch fire. Since open flames are not generally used to heat sleeping areas anymore present-day fire guard during Basic Training is more an exercise in discipline than a practical necessity, although if the weather gets cold enough some groups conducting overnight outdoor training will still use a kerosene "potbellied" stove which must be watched to prevent accidental fires. [3]

The next day the Drill Sergeants assigned positions and after they finished making an example out of me, they decided to make me a squad leader. Unfortunately, I was one of the larger individuals there and they made an example out of me to everyone what would happen if they decided to get out of line. A couple of hours after, the drills called out everyone's MOS and lined us up accordingly. I was one of three that had the MOS 09B. I asked the Drill Sergeant when was our classed going to begin.

---

[3] http://en.wikipedia.org/wiki/United_States_Army_Basic_Training

He looked at me crazy and said Boykin what are you talking about.

I told him what my recruiter told me, that every day I would go to a class in the evening, and I would be able to retake the test at a later time. The Drill Sergeant laughed and replied, Boykin get the Fu*k out of here. You are not going to any classes while in basic; your 09B is a management code for "Unassigned Trainee" as opposed to an actual MOS.

This designation means that you don't have a scheduled AIT or contracted MOS. Boykin you will be assigned your MOS "according to the needs of the Army" while in basic. But most likely you will be a mechanic, cook, or infantry man. I was furious, because my recruiter lied to me, and to top that off, I may be stuck with a MOS that I would hate. I am the last person in the world who would work on anyone's vehicle. I worked in fast-food before the military and hated that and being an infantry man wasn't in the plans.

Infantry is the branch of an army trained to fight on foot soldiers specifically trained to engage, fight, and defeat the enemy in face-to-face combat. Infantrymen thus bear the brunt of warfare, and suffer the greatest number of casualties. Historically, as the oldest branch of the combat arms, the infantry are the backbone of a modern army, and continually undergo training that is more physically stressful and demanding than that of any other branch of the combat arms, or of the army. The infantry's greater emphasis upon discipline, physical fitness, and psychological strength develops reflexive skills that enable spontaneous, sustained aggression and violence, which make a weapon-system of the infantryman, whether armed or unarmed. [4]

I would eventually be assigned the MOS of 63S. 63S is a Heavy-Wheel Vehicle Mechanic. The mechanic's duties is to perform unit maintenance on heavy-wheel vehicles (prime movers designated as more than 5 tons and their associated trailers) and material handling equipment (MHE). I also was assigned a battle buddy. He was an eighteen year old white male form Boston Massachusetts. Battle buddies are paired throughout Basic Training as a disciplinary principle whereby recruits are generally prohibited from walking anywhere alone. When recruits travel away from the platoon or drill sergeants, we are required to travel in pairs, known as battle buddies.

The training is divided up into three phases, red white, and blue. In the red phase, weeks 1-2, we begin the process of becoming soldiers; learning the Army values; working on physical fitness; learn about communications, basic first aid, map reading, and the military justice system. We also practiced drill and ceremony and negotiated Victory Tower.

---

4 *https://en.wikipedia.org/wiki/Infantry*

During Phase I or "Red Phase", also called the "Patriot phase" we were subject to "Total Control", meaning their

every action is monitored and constantly corrected by Drill Sergeants. We were often subjected to group corrective action for even minor infractions, the purpose being to develop an acute attention to detail and foster a sense of common responsibility among the unit.

Drill & Ceremony training refers to correct procedures for marching, and body movements such as standing at attention, "facing" (right-face/left-face), "at ease", "to the rear" and others. For this and many other exercises, we were sometimes issued fake rifles known as "rubber ducks", so that we could become familiar with the proper handling of our weapon.

We were also given instructions on the seven "Army Core Values," which include loyalty, duty, respect, selfless service, honor, integrity, and personal courage (meant to spell out the mnemonic LDRSHIP, or "leadership"). There are also classes held on subjects that involve day-to-day personal life in the Army, such as sexual harassment and race relations.

During week 2, we begin unarmed combat training, also known as hand-to-hand combat, Combative, or Ground Fighting Technique (GFT).We also learned how to read a map, land navigation, and compass use. These skills where put to the test at the Compass Course, where we were divided into groups and must navigate our way to a series of points throughout a wooded area.

We also had to tackle Victory Tower and the Teamwork Development Course during week 2. Victory Tower is an exercise where recruits must navigate through several obstacles at extreme heights, including climbing and traversing rope ladders and bridges. They must then rappel down a 50-foot wall (back-first, with rope harness). In the Teamwork Development Course, squads must negotiate a series of obstacles, with emphasis on working as a team rather than as individuals.

First aid training, known as Combat Life Saver (CLS), was also given during this period. We were trained in evaluating and properly treating casualties, ranging from dressing a wound to application of a tourniquet and dehydration treatment.

Weeks 3-5, is called the white phase we continued to learn about Army values and physical fitness. Much of this phase is spent learning, practicing and qualifying on the M16A2 rifle. Phase II, called the "White Phase" or "Gunfighter Phase", is where we begin actually firing weapons. With the service rifle (M16A2), we fired at various targets, which are progressively further downrange, making each successive target more difficult to hit, with additional pop-up targets at long range. Other weapons we became familiar with include various hand grenades (such as the M67), grenade launchers (such as the M203), and machine guns (such as the M240, M249, and M2).

The second week of Phase II involves familiarization with anti-tank/armor weaponry and other heavy weapons. We also learned about other U.S. military weapons, chemical warfare and bayonet training. We also participated in the obstacle course, gas chamber and bayonet assault course and have to pass another knowledge and skills test.

The blue phase, weeks 6-9, in addition to Army values and physical fitness this phase includes individual tactical techniques, foot marches, confidence course, and obstacle course.

The culmination of basic training is Victory Forge, a 7-day field training exercise combining all previously taught basic combat skills. We marched ten kilometers to our designated training site to start the exercise. We occupied a position in the field and established a defense perimeter. On subsequent days, we completed the Teamwork Reaction Course; executed tactical exercise lanes and a night tactical and live-fire exercise. The last night included a return march to the unit area and a ceremony recognizing the successful completion of this challenging operation - and the final transformation as a Soldier in the world's finest Army.

Following FTX, we then moved into the final week of training, often called "recovery week". At this time, soldiers must service and/or repair any items they are not taking on to AIT including weapons, bedding, issued equipment (helmet, canteen, gas mask, etc.) as well as ensuring the platoon barracks is in good shape to receive the next platoon of trainees. This week also included a final fitting of our dress uniform as well as practice for the graduation ceremony which takes place at the end of the week. My family came to my graduation ceremony. We were allotted to see our family for about an hour and then they put us all on a bus and shipped us to our AIT location.

Advanced Individual Training (AIT) consists of the remainder of the total Basic Training period, and is where recruits train in the specifics of their chosen field. As such, AIT is different for each available Army career path, or Military Occupational Specialty (MOS). For example, if an individual has an MOS of Human Intelligence Collector, they would be sent, following completion of BCT, to the Intelligence School at Fort Huachuca in Sierra Vista, Arizona. If an individual instead had the MOS of Army medic, they would be sent, after BCT, to the Army Medical Department School at Fort Sam Houston in San Antonio, Texas. AIT courses can last anywhere from 6 to 52 weeks. Although many AIT schools don't center on combat the way BCT does, individuals are still continually tested for physical fitness and weapons proficiency, and upon MOS, may be subject to the same duties, strict daily schedule, and disciplinary rules as in BCT. [5]

My training location was at Fort Jackson, located in South Carolina. The first phase of training, I underwent Re-integration training for the first two weeks of Core Competency training. In AIT I had certain privileges but I had to pass a knowledge exam, recite the Soldier's Creed, sing my branch song, and pass Class A, Wall Locker, and Room Inspections. Additionally, in AIT I had to demonstrate and display proper discipline, pass all academic requirements, and pass their APFT with 60 points in each event.

In AIT, we were authorized to wear civilian clothes after hours and on the weekends. We were authorized both on-post and off-post pass privileges. In some cases Company Commanders can authorize extended weekend off-post pass privileges to soldiers in AIT. All off-post passes are subject to unit recall. During extended holiday weekends, Company Commanders may authorize AIT soldiers extended overnight pass privileges. AIT soldiers were not authorized to travel further than 250 miles via POV. In AIT soldiers 21 years of age (minimum drinking age) or older were authorized on weekends and holidays to consume alcohol.

My MOS was 63S; wheeled vehicle mechanic. I was primarily responsible for supervising and performing

5 http://en.wikipedia.org/wiki/United_States_Army_Basic_Training

maintenance and recovery operations on wheeled vehicles and associated items, as well as heavy-wheeled vehicles and select armored vehicles.

I maintain wheeled vehicles, their associated trailers and material handling equipment systems inspecting, servicing, maintaining, repairing, replacement, adjusting and testing of wheeled vehicles and material handling equipment systems, subsystems and components. I was trained to service automotive electrical systems including wiring harness, and starting and charging systems and perform wheeled vehicle recovery operations

In AIT, my training for a wheeled vehicle mechanic was 13 weeks of Advanced Individual Training with on-the-job instructions. Part of this time is spent in the classroom and part in the field.

After graduating AIT and for Jackson I was granted 30 days of leave. I was able to come back to Montgomery Alabama before I had to report to Fort Hood, in Killeen, Texas. When I returned back to Montgomery, my daughter's mother decided that she wanted to try and make our relationship work. I had reservations because of everything that we had been through. However, I wanted a better situation for my daughter so I agreed.

The job security of the military allowed me to be able to purchase my first vehicle. The military movers showed up with a large eighteen wheeler and picked up all our belongings. Fort Hood is a United States military post located in Killeen, Texas. The post is named after Confederate General John Bell Hood. It is located halfway between Austin and Waco, about 60 miles from each.

The first week or so we stayed in a hotel for new soldiers and their families to the base. Eventually, I was assigned to my unit and my military career was official. During the first week of PT, I began having severe pains in my feet. These pains started in basic training, but my Drill Sergeant informed me that if they found out that something was wrong with me in basic that they would put me out of the military and I would receive nothing. He told me that if the pain continues to go to sick call when I got to my duty station.

After getting my family acclimated in our new apartment and my daughter in school, I told my First Sgt. that I was having pain in my feet and she recommended that I go to sick call and let them have a look at it. After four or five visits they discovered that I had severely damaged both Achilles tendons in both feet.

The Achilles tendon is the largest tendon in the body. It is the thick, rope-like cord on the back of the heel that connects the heel to the calf muscles. This tendon supports your entire body weight with each step. The Achilles tendon can be subjected to up to 3-12 times a person's body weight during a sudden sprint or push off.

Many things can cause injury to the Achilles tendon: Accidents, poorly chosen, ill-fitting shoes, overuse, mechanical abnormalities and misalignment (unequal leg length, short or tight Achilles tendons or calf muscles, weak calf muscles, misshapen foot or heel bones), side effects from certain medications, weak or tight calf muscles, a sudden and too-fast increase in exercise, and increasingly more powerful movements while exercising. Flat feet can also cause Achilles tendon pain. [6]

This resulted in the military assigning me a P3 profile. All Soldiers issued a permanent profile with a "3" or "4" will be referred to either the Physical Performance Evaluation System for an MMRB or the Army Physical Disability Evaluation System for an MEB (Medical Evaluation Board). My profile stated that I could not walk on uneven ground, nor could I stand in a formation, walk up or down stairs, road march, do any PT, etc. I was by Army standards, broken.

Not long after I arrived at Fort Hood, Texas, I enrolled in a local GED program at a community college. It didn't take me long to score high enough to qualify to go take the GED

---

6 http://voices.yahoo.com/understanding-achilles-tendon-pain-prevent-94609.
html?cat=70

test. I passed and received my GED on the second attempt. This was the motivation I needed. After leaving Job Corps without receiving my GED, it left me feeling like I let myself down.

Many of the sergeants in my unit thought I was faking and trying to receive something for nothing. A couple of months after I arrived at Fort Hood we received a new motor pool sergeant. Now this sergeant for whatever reason really gave me a difficult time. He would ride me, curse at me, and really talk down to me like I was beneath him. He would humiliate me in front of others, often.

The military assigned me to physical therapy this was the last step before I would be medically discharged from the Army. One day during an exercise my company was doing, this sergeant called me over and locked me up, meaning he made me stand completely still, with my hands behind my back, while he belittled me. He told me that I was a piece of sh*t. I guess that was all I could take, I felt like this was a personal attack. I told my motor pool sergeant that he was a piece of sh*t.

Due to the fact that, he was an E7 and I was an E3, I was out of order. He was a ranking officer and he eventually wrote me up causing me to receive an Article 15. Within the Uniform Code of Military Justice (UCMJ) an Article 15 provides commanders an essential tool in maintaining discipline.

The Article allows commanders to impose punishment for relatively minor infractions. Only commanders may impose punishment under Article 15. A commander is any warrant officer or commissioned officer that is in command of a unit and has been given authority, either orally or in writing, to administer non-judicial punishment.

The Article 15 brought me extra duty, and cost me rank and half my pay for 15 days. Not long after I received my out-processing papers. The next 30 days I went through a process of returning all my equipment. The military gave me a severance package and I was discharged as honorable. [7]

Types of Military Discharges

Honorable
To receive an honorable discharge, a service member must have received a rating from good to excellent for his or her service.

General
General Discharges are given to service members whose performance are satisfactory but are marked by a considerable departure in duty performance and conduct expected of military members.

---

7 http://www.armystudyguide.com/content/army_board_study_guide_topics/military_justice/about-article-15.shtml

Other than Honorable (OTH)

An OTH is the most severe form of administrative discharge. This type of discharge represents a departure from the conduct and performance expected of all military members.

Clemency Discharge

President Ford created a procedure for those military personnel who resisted against the Vietnam War to receive a Presidential Pardon and have their punitive discharges changed to a Clemency Discharge.

Bad Conduct (BCD)

A Bad Conduct Discharge (BCD) can only be given by a court-martial (either Special or General) as punishment to an enlisted service-member.

Dishonorable

A dishonorable discharge (DD) can only be handed down to an enlisted member by a general court-martial. With this characterization of service, all veterans' benefits are lost, regardless of any past honorable service, and this type of discharge is regarded as shameful in the military. [8]

On my last day in my unit the company commander called me in her office and she sat me down and she asked me, "Boykin, what are you going to do when you go back to

8 http://en.wikipedia.org/wiki/Military_discharge

Montgomery Alabama?" My reply to her was, "I don't really know."

Then she stated to me, "You will be considered a disabled veteran, which means that there are a lot of opportunities and a lot of resources available to you. She also asked me have I ever considered college. And my reply to her was, "No."

I said, "First Sgt. my mother dropped out of school, I dropped out, my sister, my brother, and my dad all dropped out and college has never really been an option for me." Then she informed me that if I decided to go to college, the Montgomery G.I. Bill would pay for me to go to college.

The Montgomery GI Bill (MGIB) is available for those who enlist in the U.S. Armed Forces. MGIB encompasses both the Montgomery GI Bill-Active Duty (Chapter 30) and The Montgomery GI Bill-Selected Reserve (Chapter 1606). Under Chapter 30, Active Duty members enroll and pay $100 per month for 12 months; and are then entitled to receive a monthly education benefit once they have completed a minimum service obligation. [9]

By this time, my daughter's mother and I really were on bad terms and decided when we get back to Montgomery, Alabama that we are going our separate ways. We packed up a U-Haul and headed back to Montgomery, Alabama.

---

[9] *http://www.gibill.va.gov/benefits/montgomery_gibill/*

CRAIG J. BOYKIN

MY LIFE, **YOUR**
INSPIRATION

**HOW TO TURN MINOR SETBACKS,
INTO A MAJOR COMEBACK!**

AN INSPIRATIONAL JOURNEY FROM GED TO PhD

The first couple of months back in Montgomery I rented a house from this nice older lady. I remember she was so excited because her deceased husband was an Army veteran. Even though my First Sergeant had spoken with me about college, by now the desire was lost. I begin looking for a job and eventually landed one at the local pawn shop. I believe my beginning wage was $5.15 per hour with the possibility for commission. My daughter's mother and I were still on bad terms and at this point I was sleeping on the couch.

One day my mother called me out of the blue and asked me to go to a beer bash with her and a friend. Initially I was hesitatant because I didn't drink, or smoke. My childhood made me develop a pure hatred for drugs and alcohol. Nevertheless, I decided to get out of the house and go. Sitting in a lawn chair at the event, I looked up and noticed one of the most attractive young ladies I had ever seen in my life.

I was so intrigued, that I decided to approach her, after several minutes of dialogue she gave me her number and we decided to go out at a later date. After going out a couple more of times Adrienne invited me to go to church with her. I was hesitant at first but I later decided to go to bible study with her. I enjoyed the church service so much that I decided that I would go back the next Sunday.

During the preachers sermon it seems as though every word that came from the pulpit was directed to me. I remember the tears trickling down my face and my heart feeling a tug. That Sunday, I decided to join church. After the service that day, it felt as though a tremendous burden had been lifted off of me.

Excited and enthusiastic, the first thing I did was go to my mother's house. I vividly remember pulling up to her house with Adrienne on that Sunday afternoon and thinking that my mother was going to be so proud of me. I told my mother that I had given my life to Christ. Her response to me was "what the fu*k are you telling me for." She told me to "Get the fu*k out of her face, I don't give a damn what you have done."

Everything that had happened to me that day instantly left and I became enraged and ended up punching a hole in her front door. After this event, I didn't speak to my mother for a while.

By this point, my daughter's mother and I had separated (although, still married). I moved into a one bedroom apartment with Adrienne. At this point the desire to go college started to fester within me again. I remembered my First Sergeant's words before I left the Army. I called the V.A. and inquired as to what steps do I need to take to enroll in college as a disabled veteran. They informed me that I qualified for a vocational rehabilitation program for disabled veteran.

The Vocational Rehabilitation and Employment (VR&E) Program sometimes referred to as Chapter 31 or Voc-Rehab, helps veterans with service-connected disabilities and employment handicaps prepare for, find, and keep suitable jobs. For veterans with service-connected disabilities so severe that they cannot immediately consider work, VR&E offers services to improve their ability to live as independently as possible.

The following services may be provided by VR&E Vet Success: Comprehensive rehabilitation evaluation to determine abilities, skills, interests, and needs. Vocational counseling and rehabilitation planning. Employment services such as job-seeking skills, resume development, and other work readiness assistance. Assistance finding and keeping a job, including the use of special employer incentives. On the Job Training (OJT), apprenticeships, and non-paid work experiences. Financial assistance for post-secondary training at a college, vocational, technical or business school. Supportive rehabilitation services including case management, counseling, and referral. Independent living services. [1]

I was given a date to report to the local Voc Rehab center. I didn't have a car at the time so the morning of I had to wake up very early and walk several miles to get to the center. I was assigned a counselor and given a new dell computer.

1 http://www.vba.va.gov/bln/vre/

After signing up for Auburn University Montgomery as a freshman they informed me that I would have to some remedial classes that wouldn't count towards me degree.

These classes are designed for individuals who may need some refreshing in these areas. I had a remedial English and remedial math class. Although all of the classes were challenging that first semester, my English class stands out to me. Being naive and not understanding college life, I scheduled myself an 8 a.m. class and regretted it the entire semester. The first day of class the professor stated that our assignment was to write a two-page paper introducing ourselves to her and the class.

I became very excited, because I knew she would be blown away by my story. After class I went to the computer lab, sat down and began to type. I was 23, a freshman in college, but this was the first time I had ever typed a paper in my life. And the fact that I didn't know how to type it took me 9 ½ hours to type a two-page paper. I printed the paper out and went back to class the following day excited.

The entire class period I was on pins and needles waiting on her to read the papers which she never did. Towards the end of class the professor asked to speak with me when the class ended. Now my nerves were really shot, I had no idea what she desired of me. After class, I approached the professor and asked her what was it that she wanted to see me about.

Her response to me was, "she didn't understand if this paper was a joke or not," offended I asked her what did she mean is this paper a joke? She stated that "this paper seems to be written not even on a fifth grade level, she stated that it was two pages of one sentence. There were no commas, no periods; it was just two continuous pages of one sentence. She stated that no real freshman in college would turn in a paper of this magnitude in a college setting. She stated that she thought I wasn't college material and maybe I needed to enroll in a community/technical college. This is when the military training kicked in and I became frustrated and I told the professor that I had overcome so much in my life that I wasn't going to start backing down now.

I have never been afraid of challenge. So I told her don't tell me what I can't do, just point me in the direction where I can get some help so that I can learn how to be successful here at Auburn University Montgomery. She gave me the number to the learning center on campus.

The goal of the Learning Center is to provide all AUM students with academic support in an inviting and dynamic environment. AUM believes that all learners need support that extends beyond the classroom to reinforce and amplify. All writers can benefit from the interaction with their writing consultants at each step on the way to paper completion, and all math students can benefit from reviewing and clarifying concepts.

The carefully selected and trained staff that work with all students from diverse backgrounds in mathematics and writing in all disciplines as well as accounting. Their trained writing consultants work with all Writing Intensive courses and provide writing and conversational instruction for English learners.[2]

I followed up by calling the number and I set up an appointment and it seems like ironically or by faith I ended up with a lady that was very nice and compassionate. I have racked my brain for numerous years trying to remember the name of the tutor that I was assigned. The first tutoring lesson we both sat down at the table and that is when she looked over the same two-page paper. I could tell immediately that she was a different kind of tutor. Although the paper was poorly written, she didn't judge me or make me feel like less of a person.

The tutor and I worked on things such as when to use elementary terms such as: too, two, to, their, there, etc. These are things that individuals learn in the third grade. But I can honestly say that this adjunct professor who was tutoring me never once looked at me as if I was ignorant. Instead she worked extremely hard with me every session. She worked with me in extra sessions that she wasn't obligated to work. Her mission was to make sure that I was equipped with the tools that I needed to be successful as a student in a university setting.

---

2 http://www.aum.edu/campus-life/student-services/learning-center

During my sophomore year in college, I saw a now hiring for mentors sign posted in a business building hallway. It paid $10 an hour, which would really help me. So I decided to call the number. I was given an interview date and eventually received the job. I was assigned three young men that were having numerous problems in school and at home. After spending countless hours with those young men, I eventually help to change the direction of their life. I became so involved that I would visit and mentor the young men even when I didn't get paid to do so.

By this time I had married my wife Adrienne Boykin and divorced my daughters mother. We were married on January 06, 2003 at the Montgomery County Court House. I became heavenly involved in the church that we were attending. I started serving as an assistant to the pastor. I would travel with him on preaching trips. I also started going to ministerial classes every Saturday.

Every Sunday the evangelist of the church would go to the local jail and attempt to encourage the inmates to change their life. After going to the jail with the evangelist for about a month he gave me an opportunity to speak to them. The response was overwhelming from the inmates. After this, the evangelist turned the responsibility of the prison ministry over to me.

The prison ministry along with the mentoring program started to uncover a skill set that I was unaware I possessed. I have the ability to inspire, and influence individuals to change for the better. Unfortunately, I had to disconnect from the pastor and the church due to several unethical things (stealing money, sleeping with women members, trickery, lying, etc.) I witnessed while serving under the senior pastor.

With a lot of hard work and dedication, I graduated from Auburn University Montgomery within three years. This was the most exciting time in my life because I didn't graduate high school so walking across that stage and receiving my diploma was very fulfilling.

After I graduated with my bachelor's degree in business administration from Auburn University Montgomery I decided to push my luck so to speak, with a Master's degree. After searching various institutions for the right degree plan, I decided to enroll at Faulkner University, pursuing a degree in theology. I graduated from Faulkner University with my Master's degree in about a year and a half. The ironic thing is that I didn't use any services offer to students with special needs.

After graduation, I began searching for something toward my next education venture. I was developing a passion for learning. At this point my brother had been incarcerated twice in prison over the last ten years and I wanted to put myself in a position to better assist him when he returned home from prison. Also through my visits at the local city jail I was becoming more involved with countless individuals who were incarcerated or involved with the criminal justice system.

So I decided to go back to Faulkner University and pursue a Master's degree in criminal justice; which in a year and a half I graduated with that degree. Still hungering with the desire to learn more, I enrolled in a Ph.D. program at Auburn University.

People often ask me "Mr. Boykin how does one go from an environment where your mother was on drugs, you having to repeat the third and fifth grade, having a learning disability and being placed in special education, dropping out a high school, shooting victim, to three college degrees and working on a fourth." My answer is always the same; **"Sheer Determination"** and I refuse to be a statistic.

My Life, My Education

Auburn University Montgomery
Bachelor's degree in Business Administration

The management specialization is designed to prepare students to respond to the opportunities and demands of a highly competitive world. The program gives students the knowledge and skills that are universally needed to be successful in leadership roles in any organization. The curriculum builds a knowledge base that includes the latest ideas in management, thought and practice, with a particular emphasis on acquiring critical people management skills.

Faulkner University
Master of Arts in Biblical Studies

The Master of Arts in Biblical Studies is the capstone of our efforts to discover and to communicate the knowledge of God's Word. With a strong Biblical core and a variety of major tracks, the Master of Arts in Biblical Studies provides both sound preparation for more effective service in the church and a broad base for further training if the student wishes to specialize in more advanced graduate study.

Faulkner University
Master of Justice Administration

The Master of Criminal Justice program is designed for those who want to advance in the field of criminal justice, enter it, or simply gain a deeper understanding of this fascinating discipline. A degree in Criminal Justice will give you a competitive edge whether you plan to enhance your career, teach, apply to law school, or pursue a doctorate. Degree candidates will take courses where they will analyze criminal behavior, apply principles of leadership in organizational settings, learn theories of social control, and gain an informed perspective of law enforcement, the judicial system, and corrections. Ever evolving and often misunderstood, crime and justice are central to the moral fabric and social cohesion of society.

Auburn University
Ph.D. in Adult Education

The Adult Education program prepares students for careers in adult education fields, such as business and industry trainers, college and university faculty, teachers of Adult Basic Education, independent training consultants, educational program writers and evaluators, individuals with special interests or expertise offering sessions through community or educational agencies, conducting evening adult classes, community leadership positions, and authors of self-help books.

CHAPTER VII
My Life, the Future is Bright

CRAIG J. BOYKIN

MY LIFE, **YOUR**
INSPIRATION

HOW TO TURN MINOR SETBACKS, INTO A MAJOR COMEBACK!

AN INSPIRATIONAL JOURNEY FROM GED TO PhD

Today I am considered one of the nation's leading authorities in understanding and stimulating human potential, utilizing a powerful delivery and newly emerging insights to teach, inspire and channel people to new levels of achievement. My personal mission in life is to provide hope to individuals who feel that their current situation is hopeless. I travel the country presenting his seminar, "Make Life Count".

In 2006, I started an organization by the name of 180 Group. The mission of 180 Group is to provide hope to individual who feel hopeless; to ensure that every individual has the same opportunity regardless of his/her past, criminal status, and current economic or social status. The organization never officially became a 501c3 because at the time I didn't have the capital. Therefore, I was never able to receive any, grants, donations or contributions from individuals, businesses or the government. Everything I did came out of my own personal resources. 180 Group was the launching pad for speaking at numerous speaking engagements.

In 2013, after a conference call with Nadine Lee, (Speak the Dream - Los Angeles), Sandra Denice Newton, Tony Nix (Enough is Enough, New York), Diane Latiker (Kids off the block, Chicago), and myself, the idea of United Dream Montgomery was birthed. United Dream Montgomery seeks to empower individuals to live a life of hope, integrity and compassion while making positive changes in their lives, communities and the world.

United Dream Montgomery's vision is to rally communities to combat the infectious activities (behaviors) that plague our youth, communities, families, educators, and educational institutions.

Adrienne Boykin (My wife)

When I met my wife, she was doing hair as a cosmetologist. Some years later she grew weary of this decade long career. She decided to go back to school to pursue and career as an educator. She graduated from Faulkner University with a Bachelor's Degree in Elementary Education and is proud to serve as the 2nd Grade Reading Teacher for Jackson Steele Elementary in Lowndes County. Adrienne was the recipient of the Elementary Education Award and is a proud member of Kappa Delta Pi (National Educator's Honor Society).

Adrienne believes that the purpose of an educator is to aid children in developing their own knack for success in life. An educator should seek to identify and address the particular learning style, talent, interest, and need of each child. Adrienne further believes that all students have the potential to learn, even though not all children learn at the same rate or in the same manner.

Not only does Adrienne aspire to expose students to various ideas, methods, and strategies that will be of assistance to them throughout their educational process, she aspires to mold every student into a "lifelong learner." There is one quote, by William Arthur Ward that sums up everything Adrienne believes teaching entails; "The mediocre teacher tells. The good teacher explains. The superior teacher demonstrates. "The great teacher inspires."

My Brother

My brother went to prison at the early age of 17 and was released at 21. Six months after being released my brother returned to prison a second time with a 10 and 15 year sentence. He went back to prison for seven more years and was released in 2012 on parole. He will be on parole until 2025, being on parole means that my brother can return to prison under the three strikes law at any given time and would have to serve a life sentence. Currently, my brother has resisted temptation and is currently working as an overnight stocker at Wal-Mart.

My Mother

My mother got off of drugs around the time I was 13 and stayed off for many years. She went to Trenholm State Technical College and received an associate degree or certificate in early care and education not sure which one. She got a job working at a local head start program as a teacher. She has worked at this job for the last 15-20 years.

My relationship with my mother got progressively worse over time. It seemed to me the more productive I became the more we grew apart. One of the most hurtful events of my life was when my brother was released from prison the first time. My mother, with tears in her eyes, ran over and threw her arms around him and told him that she was so proud of him and that she loved him. I can only remember one instance in my life when my mother told me that she loved me and I initiated the response. One day out of the blue I called my mother and told her that I loved her and I didn't hold her accountable for my upbringing. I understood that she was a product of her environment. She replied that she loved me too, but it was very cold and dry, nothing like what she had exhibited that day with my brother.

The beginning of the end, so to speak was when my grandmother who raised me died in New York. My other grandmother made the suggestion that we (me, my wife, my mother, sister and brother) all pile in her escalade and drive to the funeral in New York. My mother told my grandmother that if I was going, she wouldn't get in the car with my motherfuc*ing as*. So my grandmother told her that Craig is going, so I guess you're not.

Outside of a phone conversation with my brother and sister, I would have never thought that my mother would ever use drugs again. Then one day, I get a phone call from my grandmother stating that I need to come over to her house immediately. What I found when I got to her house would set me back 15 years. My mother had been using my grandmother's debit card and bank account to pay her own utility bills for the past 12 months.

This started a feud within the family and immediately divided everyone. My grandmother had no choice but to press charges on my mother. Eventually, she confessed to everyone that she was back on drugs, and was using my grandmother's account to pay her bills and she spent about 70-80 dollars a week on her drug habit. My mother was charged with two felonies. She is currently on a Pre-Trial Diversion (PTD) Program. PTD diverts certain first-time nonviolent defendants from the traditional court system into a highly individualized and supervised restorative program.

My mother will be required to work, further her educational training, perform volunteer work weekly, participate in counseling, report to the PTD Office, and pay restitution to my grandmother.

If my mother successfully completes the program, the case will not be brought to trial. The District Attorney will file a Motion to nolle pros the case, and there will not be a conviction. However, if my mother does not complete the PTD program, she will be sentenced as they would for any other conviction. My mother and I have not spoken now for some time. My mother has told me that had she known about abortions when she was pregnant with me, I wouldn't be here today. She has also told me that I am dead to her on many occasions.

My mother recently told me that if she dies don't come to her funeral and if I die she would spit on my grave. She has threatened to sue me for defamation numerous times also.

My Sister

We haven't spoken in a year at the time this book was written.

My Father

My father lives in Conyers, GA. He is married with two boys David and Christian. We have made several attempts to reconcile our relationship but each time has resulted in failure.

CRAIG J. BOYKIN

MY LIFE, **YOUR**
INSPIRATION

**HOW TO TURN MINOR SETBACKS,
INTO A MAJOR COMEBACK!**

AN INSPIRATIONAL JOURNEY FROM GED TO PhD

Remember, you and you alone must decide to act at any moment. This moment is your golden opportunity to break away from the limitations of the past, and to live and act with a positive resolve. You must stop worrying about what has happened in the past, the opportunities you have let slip by, or the hurt that others may have imposed on you, for there is nothing you can do now to undo what has already happened. But you do have the power, at this very moment, to change your life for the better. Any day you wish, you can discipline yourself to change it all.

Failure isn't failure, if you learn something from it; it's only failure if you fail to learn anything from it! It's sad that we are conditioned to blame others for our lack of motivation to change! Live your life now. Do not wait; the time will never be just right! Start where you stand, and work with whatever tools you may have at your command, and better tools will be found as you go along.

Everyone has two paths they can take in life, the first path is filled with familiarity and leads to the same old places you have been before, and the other path is filled with uncertainty, but can lead you to many new and exciting places! Many people don't choose the second path for they fear the unknown, therefore they accept things that are routine or common and refuse to grow!

You can have whatever you dream, as long as you stop dreaming at some point and start applying applications and principals to achieve that dream! There will be a moment today that affords you the opportunity to transform into something great, what you will do in that moment capture greatness or settle for less, seize the moment when it happens!

The only people that are ashamed of their past, are the ones that haven't come into the understanding of their future! You are only one choice away from being the person you always dreamed of being!

In the middle of difficulty, lies opportunity, I believe that difficult situations present an opportunity for you to transform into something great. Life is a journey for all of us, from birth through the stages of life until death, we are faced with a series of experiences; some wonderful and joyful, others challenging and difficult. As I look back over my life I can see that it is fairly typical of this pattern, I am also aware that the harder places have afforded real opportunities for change.

God promises to be with us in the difficult places, but does not promise to lift us out of them. He knows that difficulties can cause us to grow and change and ultimately be for our good.

There are two types of mistakes: those that you can learn from, and those that can change the entire scope of your life forever and may be irreversible!

- Unknown Author

CHAPTER IX
My Life, **Forgotten Stories**

CRAIG J. BOYKIN

MY LIFE, **YOUR**
INSPIRATION

**HOW TO TURN MINOR SETBACKS,
INTO A MAJOR COMEBACK!**

AN INSPIRATIONAL JOURNEY FROM GED TO PhD

This section of the book revisits events in my life that were forgotten until the completion of this book.

Floating Across the Water

I sucked a baby pacifier until I was five. My two older cousins from Chicago would come to Alabama every summer and have a field day picking on me. In typical older cousin fashion they terrorized me. One day while playing around my grandmother's water pond, they decided to put me in a card board box and float me across the water. Lucky for me, as soon as they put the box in the water it immediately began to sink.

Stole a Car from church

Somewhere around the age of 14 my grandmother started allowing me to drive her car different places. One of these places was to church on Sunday morning. She became so comfortable that she started allowing me to keep her car keys during church service. One day during a church service, me and a couple of friend's from church, along with my brother made the decision to take my grandmothers car joy riding. I was driving; the music was blasting so loud I couldn't even hear myself think. Not paying attention to what I was doing I almost hit a police car in the process. I remember thinking that this was about to get real bad. The officer just looked at me and pulled off. I could tell that he was really pissed off, but I was elated that he didn't pull me over and take me to jail.

New Neighborhood

After my mother met the guy she would eventually wed we moved to a neighborhood entitled brickdale. This neighborhood was infested with Crips, a local gang. The Crips are one of the largest gangs in the United States. Founded in Los Angeles during the late 1960s, the Crips gang developed and rose in strength due to the breakdown in the community leadership of the African American community following the LA riots. [1] The Crip gang started recruiting my brother and me very strongly. The first day at our new school, a group of Crips walked up to me and asked me if I was in a gang. This was all new to me, and I guess I answered the question incorrectly because they leader slapped me in the face. This pissed me off, and as I attempted to retaliate about 20 other Crips jumped up ready to fight me. This would happen almost daily. They were using intimidation and fear to recruit me.

During one bullying experience a guy who was sixteen in the six grade pulled out a knife on the school bus and said that he was going to stab me. Eventually, the bus driven made it to my neighborhood and I was able to make it to my house. After about 15 minutes of pushing back in forth in my front

---

1 *http://gangs.umd.edu/Gangs/Crips.aspx*

yard between me, my brother and about 15 Crips we were able to go into the house. I guess they refused to concede to the front door being locked because they begin to kick, punch, throw thing at the door. I called my mother and she told me to call the police. These types of bullying experiences lasted the entire school year.

Doing Homework

One day while I was sitting in the bedroom doing homework, a random guy who was very intoxicated came in our house attempting to use the rest room. I guess his state wouldn't allow for that to happen, because halfway to the bathroom, he just unzipped his pants and started urinating right there in front of me on the floor.

The Phone Call That Could Have Ended It All

One day I received a phone call from one of my classmates. This was strange to me because we were friends, but we had never conversed via the telephone. He expressed his concern over a conversation that he overheard a mutual friend having regarding me. A couple of guys were planning to rob me. The ring leader of the conversation was my best friend in seven grade, but eventually moved to a different school. The caller said that the plan was to have my ex-best friend call me late one night and say that he was stranded in a local housing project that only had one way in and one way out.

Once I drove into the housing project they all were going to rob me at gun point and take my car. Ironically, I received a phone call later that night just has he had described, but I refused to go!!!

My Life, **Timeline**

1979 – Born

1986 - Diagnosed With A Learning Disability And Placed In Special Education Classes

1987 – Repeated The Third Grade

1989 - Repeated The Fifth Grade

1997 – Dropped Out Of School Unable To Write A Five Sentence Paragraph

1998 – Shot Because Of Gang Activities

1998 – Trouble With The Legal System

1999 – Daughter Was Born

1999 – Enroll In The Job Corps In Prestonsburg, KY

2000 – Received My Diploma In Retail Sales

2000 – Joined The Military

2001 - Received My GED

2003 – Enrolled In College At Auburn University Montgomery

2003 – Became A Baptized Believer In Jesus Christ

2003 – Married My Wife (Adrienne Boykin)

2005 – Starting Mentoring Other Misguided Young Men

2006 – Started Public Speaking

2006 - Graduated From Auburn University Montgomery With My Bachelor's Degree

2008 – Started A Nonprofit (180 Group) To Help Others Overcome Their Situations

2010 – Graduated From Faulkner University With A
      Master Degree In Theology

2013 – Graduated From Faulkner University With My 2nd
      Master Degree In Criminal Justice

2013 – Started United Dream Montgomery

2013 – Enrolled in a Ph.D. Program At Auburn University
      (War Eagle) In Adult Education

2013 – Published my First Book: "My Life,
      Your Inspiration"

2014 – Unlimited

2015 – Unlimited

2016 – Unlimited

Delivering the keynote address at the Bevill State Community College commencement ceremony.

Delivering an inspirational message to at-risk males in the Atlanta area.

Inner City Evangelism partnering with United Dream Montgomery at a local housing community.

3on3 Shoot Out the Violence Basketball Tournament with the Mayor of Montgomery, Todd Strange.

3on3 Shoot Out the Violence Basketball Tournament with over 250 in attendance at this inaugural event.

Picture with Sue H. Edge, Program Director at Lee County Literacy Coalition after a GED graduation keynote speech.

My Life, **Quotes**

Behind every fact is a face. Behind every statistic is a story. Behind every catch phrase is a young person whose future will be lost if something is not done immediately to change his or her reality.

- Unknown Author

My Life, **Quotes**

Remember that ignorance is learned; therefore one has to unlearn the ignorance that has been introduced to them before they can grow, or stop doing destructive behaviors!

- Unknown Author

My Life, **Quotes**

Generational Ignorance is the worse, because to the individuals who are exhibiting the ignorance, in most cases they don't see anything wrong with their actions, because these actions have been integrated into their value system as normal, because this is what they saw or was taught as normal!

– Unknown Author

My Life, **Quotes**

The continuous exodus of young Black males from their communities to the prison systems destabilizes the black communities in many ways!

– Unknown

You were born a "priceless" original, and if you're not careful life will make you just another "useless" copy!
~ Craig J. Boykin